ADAPTED FROM SISTERS IN SPIRIT

We Want Equal Rights!

How Suffragists Were Influenced by Haudenosaunee Women

SALLY ROESCH WAGNER

7th Generation
SUMMERTOWN, TENNESSEE

Library of Congress Cataloging-in-Publication Data available on request.

Brief quotations appearing in this book have been taken from the following sources:

R. Emerson and Russell P. Dobash, "Wives: The 'Appropriate' Victims of Marital Violence," *Victimology: An International Journal* 2 (1977–78): pp. 430–431.

Elizabeth Cady Stanton, *The Matriarchate or Mother-Age,* National Council of Women of the United States. Transactions of the National Council Women of the United States: 1891, pp. 218–227.

Alice Fletcher, "The Legal Conditions of Indian Women," pp. 238–239. National Woman Suffrage Association, Washington, D.C. Evening Session (29 Mar 1888).

Emma Vignal Borglum, The Experience at Crow Creek: A Sioux Indian Reservation at South Dakota. Collection of the Manuscript Division, Library of Congress.

Matilda Joslyn Gage, *Woman, Church and State,* Chicago: Charles Kerr, 1893; reprint ed., Aberdeen, South Dakota: Sky Carrier Press, 1998.

Matilda Joslyn Gage, "Indian Citizenship," National Citizen and Ballot Box, May 1878.

We chose to print this title on sustainably harvested paper stock certified by the Forest Stewardship Council, an independent auditor of responsible forestry practices. For more information, visit us.fsc.org.

© 2020 Sally Roesch Wagner

Printed in the United States of America

7th Generation
an imprint of Book Publishing Company
PO Box 99, Summertown, TN 38483
888-260-8458
bookpubco.com
nativevoicesbooks.com

ISBN: 978-1-939053-28-2

25 24   2 3 4 5 6 7 8 9

Contents

Acknowledgments

I am grateful that Kathie Hanson has adapted my 2011 book, *Sisters in Spirit: Haudenosaunee (Iroquois) Influence on Early American Feminists,* making it accessible to a young audience. While she followed the book closely, there are some changes with more appropriate language and content corresponding to my later scholarship.

Kathie has wisely chosen to position the book in commemoration of the one-hundredth anniversary of the Nineteenth Amendment, which placed in the Constitution the federal government's guarantee to protect women citizens in their right to vote. Given voter suppression today, we still have work to do, requiring the federal government to live up to its promise. May this book inspire you to become part of that responsibility to the women who come after us, just as our suffrage foremothers fought for the right for us.

Sally Roesch Wagner

Creating a More Inclusive History

History is created by people, but often that history is told through the eyes of the people in charge. Until recently, U.S. history was centered on white males and was told from their point of view. It supported the idea that wars are the most important events in history and that the only people who matter are white men—especially wealthy ones.

Reflecting the cultural and social shifts of the last half century, our nation's history now includes more stories of diversity. As various groups began to demand their civil rights during the 1960s, they also demanded to tell their versions of history. People of color, women, children, gay men and lesbians, and poor people told various stories of injustice.

Throughout history, oppressed people survived seemingly impossible situations and demanded improvements in their conditions. Courage and strength of spirit are shown by their stories. For example, despite being enslaved, African Americans maintained their honor, their family ties, and a sense of community.

Most recently, we have begun to explore the largely unknown stories of how friendships during colonial times created avenues of influence among Indigenous peoples and European colonists. The fact that the founding fathers of our country modeled their newly formed government on that of the Six Nations (Iroquois) is a fascinating example. Native influence on the non-Native women's rights movement is another story of friendship and inspiration—one I hope will reveal possibilities for your own life.

—Sally Roesch Wagner

"Let all government cease from off the face of the earth, if we cannot build up a government of equality. A rebel! How glorious the name sounds when applied to woman. Oh, rebellious woman, to you the world looks in hope. Upon you has fallen the glorious task of bringing liberty to the earth and all the inhabitants thereof."

MATILDA JOSLYN GAGE

Chapter 1

The Condition of Women Before Social Change

When we look at the social standing of women in the mid-1800s, we can understand the need for change. For instance, we take wearing clothes that are attractive, comfortable, and serviceable for granted, but 150 years ago, women's clothing was very restrictive. Women were covered from neck to foot; heaven forbid that a woman's ankle was seen! Corsets, bonnets, and gloves were standard attire.

A married woman was considered dead in the eyes of the law. She lost her name, any right to control her own body, and the ability to live where she chose. She could not enter into any contracts, sue someone, or be sued. In return, she was entitled to honor and respect; nothing more. Legal scholars of the day agreed that women should be honored and respected but were not entitled to more consideration than that. A single woman might own property, earn a living, and be economically independent, but after saying her marriage vows, she lost control of her property and her earnings to her new husband. All rights to the children she would bear automatically went to him as well. Her children actually became the property of the father.

Bloomers

The women of the religious reform Oneida Community were among the first to dramatically alter their restrictive clothing. At that time, society dictated that women wear many layers of heavy undergarments, as well as dangerously tight, deforming corsets. They refused to wear twenty pounds of the clothing that was in style at the time and in 1848 adopted the "bloomer," a short dress and leggings like those worn by North America's Indigenous peoples. Other women followed, leading to a dress reform movement.

Most states gave men so much legal power over their children that a dying man with a pregnant wife could select another man to be the owner of their unborn child. That man could take the baby away from the mother who had just given birth to it—based on the law that the child had to be cared for by its "legal owner."

With the words "I do," a woman literally gave up her legal identity. Even when a woman found herself in a loving marriage with a caring husband, she was completely under his control. Until property laws protecting married women were slowly enacted state by state, any money or material goods a wife brought into the marriage or earned belonged outright to her husband.

The law allowed wife beating. A husband had the right to beat his wife as long as the battering wasn't "too harsh," and U.S. courts generally upheld that right.

For example, in an 1864 case in North Carolina, a husband and wife had separated, but he entered the home, grabbed her by her hair, pulled her onto the floor, and held her there, injuring her head and throat. The pain she endured continued for several months after the attack. The North Carolina Supreme Court affirmed the husband's right to do so in the following ruling:

> A husband is responsible for the acts of his wife, and he is required to govern his household, and for that purpose the law permits him to use towards his wife such a degree of force as is necessary to control an unruly temper and make her behave herself, and unless some permanent injury be inflicted, or there be an excess of violence, or such a

Nineteenth-century married couple

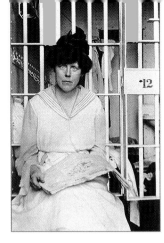

Suffragist Lucy Burns in jail after protesting at the White House in 1917

Katherine Morey, an American suffragist, under arrest after protesting in Boston in 1917

degree of cruelty as show that it is inflicted to gratify his own bad passions, the law . . . prefers to leave the parties to themselves, as the best mode of inducing them to make the matter up and live together as man and wife should.

Christian leaders generally held the opinion that marriage was a covenant with God that no woman had a right to break, even if her life was in danger from a violent husband. Thanks to early equal rights activists, divorce laws slowly began to change in the late 1800s, but many women still found themselves trapped and unable to get away from violent or abusive husbands. If a wife was desperate enough to run away from a dangerous husband, she could be returned to him by the police, just as an enslaved person escaping to freedom would be returned to their master.

Women Need Votes
TO GET STRINGENT
URE FOOD LAWS

MOTHERS
PREPARE THE CHILDREN FOR THE WORLD
PREPARE THE WORLD FOR THE CHILDREN

Suffrage Pioneers
NEED FOR MARRIED WOMEN
THE RIGHT TO
THEIR CHILDREN

RALLY!
FOR THE
WOMAN
SUFFRAGE
AMENDMENT

Suffragists on the march in Washington, DC, in 1917, demanding their rights

Men controlled all the means of employment and whatever wages a woman might be able to make through the limited work available to her, perhaps by being a teacher (if unmarried; married women were not allowed to teach), doing laundry for another family, or selling the produce from her garden. Women were also prohibited from attaining a higher education and becoming a professor, preacher, doctor, or lawyer. Because they couldn't vote, they couldn't hold public office, and they certainly were denied entry into the business world. The time was ripe for change, and more women wanted their rights.

"We are assembled to protest against a form of government, existing without the consent of the governed" to declare our right to be free as man is free, to be represented in the government which we are taxed to support, to have such disgraceful laws as give man the power to chastise and imprison his wife, to take the wages which she earns, the property which she inherits, and, in case of separation, the children of her love."

ELIZABETH CADY STANTON

Chapter 2

The Early Suffragists

The word "suffrage" means "the right to vote." When the United States was founded, only white males who owned land had the right to vote (although a few women voted in some of the colonies if they owned land) because the framers of the Constitution felt that owning property made people more responsible. Over the next fifty years, some individual states granted men who did not own land the right to vote, but state restrictions continued to limit the vote to rich, white men. Things changed when the first section of the 1868 Fourteenth Amendment declared that "all persons born or naturalized in the United States . . . are citizens of the United States" with "equal protection of the laws." However, the second section defined citizens as male only, implying that women were not citizens with rights. In 1870, the Fifteenth Amendment granted any man the right to vote, regardless of race or color, but women were still constitutionally barred from the voting booth.

Although a number of women fostered the early women's rights movement, three in particular have a unique story to tell. Elizabeth Cady Stanton, Lucretia Coffin Mott, and Matilda Joslyn Gage were early founders of the movement advocating for rights, privileges, and protections

9

Elizabeth Cady Stanton

Lucretia Coffin Mott

for women. These three activists fought for the same demands that many women make today: the control of their property and earnings, equal pay for equal work, and an end to abusive marriage. They were labeled "suffragists" because they formed the first major women's rights organizations focusing on the vote after the Fifteenth Amendment extended the ballot to all men.

Elizabeth Cady Stanton

An outstanding student, Elizabeth Cady (1815–1902) graduated in 1832 from the Troy Female Seminary, the first school in the nation to provide higher education for young women on the same level as that given to young men.

During visits to her cousin, the social reformer Gerrit Smith, she became drawn to the abolition movement. In 1840, she married the noted Henry Stanton, and she omitted the word "obey" from her marriage vows. On their honeymoon, they traveled to London so Henry could attend the World Anti-Slavery Convention, to which he had been elected a delegate. The male delegates voted to exclude the official women delegates from the United States from participating in the proceedings. Elizabeth sat with those women, including Lucretia Coffin Mott, behind a curtain where they had been confined.

Lucretia Coffin Mott

Lucretia Coffin Mott (1793–1880) was raised a Quaker, a religion that stresses equality of all people under God, and she attended a Quaker boarding school in upstate New York. In 1809, the family moved to Philadelphia, and two years later, Mott married her father's business partner, James Mott, with whom she had six children.

Mott and her husband were abolitionists and attended the World Anti-Slavery Convention in London in 1840 as official delegates of their anti-slavery organizations. While James took part, Lucretia was silenced with the other women delegates.

These rejected women were inspired to action by their exclusion. Working for the rights of the enslaved, they themselves were treated

SENECA FALLS CONVENTION

The 1848 Seneca Falls Convention, held in Seneca Falls, New York, was the first local women's rights convention in the United States. The purpose of the convention was to work for the social, civil, and religious rights of women. Their "Declaration of Sentiments" outlined the many ways that men had established tyranny over women.

The convention voted to pass eleven resolutions on women's rights, such as the right of women to seek employment as they saw fit, that they were the equals of men in every way, and that they could write or speak publicly and fervently about their beliefs. Sadly, all these resolutions passed unanimously except for the one that demanded the right for women to vote. It was thought so controversial that it might jeopardize adoption of the declaration as a whole.

DECLARATION OF SENTIMENTS

When, in the course of human events,
it becomes necessary for one portion of the family of man
to assume among the people of the earth
a position different from that which they have hitherto occupied,
but one to which the laws of nature
and of nature's God entitle them,
a decent respect to the opinions of mankind requires
that they should declare the causes
that impel them to such a course.

We hold these truths to be self-evident:
that all men and women are created equal;
that they are endowed by their Creator
with certain inalienable rights;
that among these are life, liberty, and the pursuit of happiness;
that to secure these rights governments are instituted,
deriving their just powers from the consent of the governed—
Whenever any form of Government
becomes destructive of these ends,
it is the right of those who suffer from it to refuse allegiance to it,

and to insist upon the institution of a new government,
laying its foundation on such principles,
and organizing its powers in such form as to them shall seem
most likely to effect their safety and happiness.
Prudence, indeed, will dictate that governments long established
should not be changed for light and transient causes;
and accordingly, all experience hath shown
that mankind are more disposed to suffer, while evils are sufferable,
than to right themselves by abolishing
the forms to which they are accustomed.
But when a long train of abuses and usurpations,
pursuing invariably the same object,
evinces a design to reduce them under absolute despotism,
it is their duty to throw off such government,
and to provide new guards for their future security.
Such has been the patient sufferance
of the women under this government,
and such is now the necessity which constrains them
to demand the equal station to which they are entitled.

National Women's Rights Conventions

When Lucretia Coffin Mott visited Quaker abolitionists in Waterloo, New York, in the summer of 1848, they invited Elizabeth Cady Stanton to come from nearby Seneca Falls to join them. Visiting over tea, the women were determined to call a women's rights convention such as they had discussed in London eight years before.

The people who attended the Seneca Falls Convention hoped they could inspire women and men in other parts of the country to form their own meetings to discuss the rights of women. This led to the calling of a series of first local meetings and then National Women's Rights Conventions, which were held every year except one during the 1850s. A broad range of women's issues was discussed, from marriage reform and equal pay to opportunities in education and in the workplace, along with the right of women to vote.

YE MAY SESSION OF YE WOMAN'S RIGHTS CONVENTION—YE ORATOR OF YE DAY DENOUNCING YE LORDS OF CREATION.

An illustration mocking a Women's Rights Convention in 1859 that accurately depicts the unruly crowd of spectators

like second-class citizens. The delegates took advantage of the opportunity to talk about women's rights with the other women attendees and formulated a plan to bring back to the U.S.

Matilda Joslyn Gage

Matilda Joslyn Gage (1826–1898) grew up in a home that was an active station on the Underground Railroad—a network of abolitionists who helped enslaved people escape to freedom.

She attended two years of higher education at the coeducational Clinton Liberal Institute. Her dream of going on to medical school ended when she was denied entrance to Geneva Medical School, despite her physician father's intervention.

In 1845 Matilda married Henry Hill Gage, and they raised four children. Gage did not attend the local Seneca Falls Convention in 1848, but she joined the movement, along with Susan B. Anthony, four years later at the third National Women's Rights Convention held in nearby Syracuse, New York. She quickly became a regular organizer of meetings and conventions, local and national, while speaking at both. In addition to speaking throughout the state on women's rights, she began her prolific publication career, writing stories and newspaper articles on the subject.

Gage became part of the leadership of the National Woman Suffrage Association, along with Stanton and Anthony, for the twenty years of the organization, from 1869 to 1889. She dropped out of the organized movement when a merger between the progressive National Woman Suffrage Association and the more conservative American Woman Suffrage Association changed the direction of the movement. Of the three women—Stanton, Gage, and Mott—Gage was the most progressive. Along with Stanton, she criticized Christianity and the Christian church for its deep-rooted preaching of women as inferior and subservient to men. She carried a vision far beyond equality to the total destruction of the institutional inequality of people.

Matilda Joslyn Gage

Susan B. Anthony

As an Indian woman I was free. I owned my home, my person, the work of my own hands, and my children should never forget me. I was better as an Indian woman than under white law.

AN OMAHA NATION WOMAN SPEAKING TO ALICE FLETCHER

Chapter 3

The Influence of the Six Nations

We know that Stanton, Gage, and Mott worked to gain equal rights for women, but who influenced these women? They lived in a male-dominated society. The surprising reply is the Haudenosaunee (Haw-de-no-saw-nee), the People of the Longhouse. "Iroquois," which is the popular non-Native term for them today, was a designation used by the French fur traders who first did business with them. These people, whose original land base covered all of New York State and then went up into Canada and down into Pennsylvania, formed a peace confederacy over a thousand years ago on the shores of Onondaga Lake, in present-day Syracuse, New York. The Mohawk, Oneida, Onondaga, Cayuga, and Seneca Nations came together to form the Six Nations Confederacy, later adding the Tuscarora Nation.

What Was the Six Nations Confederacy?

The citizens of the Six Nations Confederacy enjoyed peace among themselves, along with equality and a harmony and balance with nature and the earth long before the Europeans arrived. They signed treaties

Left: Haudenosaunee girls take part in Ohero:kon rites-of-passage ceremony with their moms (2019). From left to right: Kanatires, Katsistohkwineh, Lenenharihshon, Lonatarishon, Katsi'tsi:io, Dylan.

Haudenosaunee longhouse

Haudenosaunee family

and traded, and also assisted and instructed the Europeans who were settling among them. Despite the scorched-earth policy of the Sullivan-Clinton campaign during the Revolutionary War and the subsequent taking of much of the Six Nations' land, it is amazing that cultural sharing and even friendship sometimes formed between North America's Indigenous people and settlers. Matilda Joslyn Gage lived in, Elizabeth Cady Stanton grew up in, and Lucretia Coffin Mott visited the villages and towns that developed in the Six Nations' territory. All three of these leading suffragists knew Six Nations women and had dealings with them.

"Among the Iroquois, the women had the veto power in war, and Sir Wm. Johnson reports an instance where the Mohawk women forbade the young braves going to battle . . . But an American woman can say nothing . . . Her consent is not asked, she has no part nor lot in the matter but to suffer. Some men say that women, if they held the ballot, would drive the country into war at their will, whereas the fact is we shall never have a peace government until woman has a recognized voice upon the question."

MATILDA JOSLYN GAGE

Daily life around a
Haudenosaunee longhouse

Women's Role in Six Nations Society

Six Nations women were farmers. What an amazing fact this must have
been to women who were supposed to be corseted and fashionably weak
and were believed to be incapable of hard labor! Most white women
were resigned to their place inside the home, but not Native women.
Gage marveled at their highly effective and unique methods of farm-
ing, unknown to white men.

Haudenosaunee family

In an Indigenous field, the sod was not turned with a plow,
Gage reflected. The traditional Native method was to "tickle the
ground with a hoe" until it "laughed with a harvest."

Six Nations women planted primarily corn, beans, and squash
in mounds. The combination is ecologically sound. The cornstalk
provides support for the beans, while the beans provide nitro-
gen to nourish the corn. The squash covers the mound, keeping
weeds out and moisture in. Eaten together, these "Three Sup-
porters" or "Three Sisters," as they were called, provided the
staple of their diet.

The Role of Newspapers

The women who initiated the women's rights movement in the late 1800s obviously could not communicate through phones, email, texts, or social media, nor could they watch television. The only avenues available to them for reaching the public were speaking, writing letters, and publishing newspaper articles. At that time, reading newspapers was the principal way that people learned about the world around them.

Newspapers provided a wide range of information on the Six Nations. One hundred years ago, even the average person in upstate New York would have known a great deal about these Nations. Newspapers assumed, for example, that the readers knew the process by which a chief was chosen. The local Syracuse paper, the *Onondaga Standard*—which Gage read—reported everything from Six Nations' condolence ceremonies, in which a new chief was installed, to council meetings and spiritual ceremonies. When a New York law was proposed to break up the communal land of the Six Nations and create individual ownership rights, the protests of the Onondaga Nation, one of the Six Nations, were published in full by the newspaper, along with the names of all the signatures on the petitions to save their land.

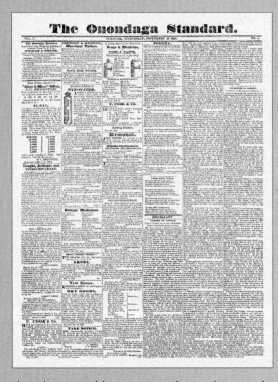

When Gage, Stanton, and Mott picked up their local or national newspapers, they were able to gain general knowledge about the Six Nations and read the current news about their society. From their school textbooks to local and national histories and popular novels, knowledge of Native Americans was also prevalent. It is not surprising that when reformers like Gage looked for a model for their vision of an equal society, they quickly found their well-known Indigenous neighbors. What was revealed to them about the status of Six Nations women in their Nations?

In 1875, while serving as president of the National Woman Suffrage Association, Gage penned a series of admiring articles about the Six Nations for the *New York Evening Post* in which she wrote about the equal sharing of power between the men and women of the Six Nations Confederacy and how the structure of their family life showed how the women's authority was honored.

In a similar article also published at that time in the *Post*, Gage recognized the superiority of the Native women's agricultural method. She believed the Six Nations' recognition of the spiritual, life-giving supremacy of women's ability to create food represented a higher form of civilization than her own. She also noted that in Christian Europe during the Middle Ages, farmers had a very low position in society, and the warrior was the aristocrat of civilization. Gage felt that the very opposite should be the case.

Among the responsibilities of Six Nations women, balanced by those of the men, was overseeing the home and the land, as well as the community's agriculture. Both satisfying and sacred, women's work

NATIONAL WOMAN SUFFRAGE ASSOCIATION

After the Civil War, the abolition and women's rights movements joined together to work for universal suffrage—the vote for everyone. However, the Fifteenth Amendment gave the right to vote only to Black men. Determined that women should have equal citizenship with men, Gage, Stanton, and Mott joined other women to establish the National Woman Suffrage Association in 1869. This organization submitted a women's suffrage draft to Congress that eventually became the Nineteenth Amendment to the Constitution, granting women the right to vote.

The Nineteenth Amendment to the U.S. Constitution

PASSED BY CONGRESS JUNE 4, 1919. RATIFIED AUGUST 18, 1920

The right of citizens of the United States to vote shall not be denied or abridged by the United States or by any State on account of sex.
Congress shall have power to enforce this article by appropriate legislation.

SAVAGERY TO "CIVILIZATION"

DRAWN BY JOSEPH KEPPLER

THE INDIAN WOMEN: We whom you pity as drudges reached centuries ago the goal that you are now nearing

WE, THE WOMEN OF THE IROQUOIS:
Own the land, the lodge, the children.
Ours is the right of adoption, of life or death;
Ours the right to raise up and depose chiefs;
Ours the right of representation at all councils;
Ours the right to make and abrogate treaties;
Ours the supervision over domestic and foreign policies;
Ours the trusteeship of the tribal property;
Our lives are valued again as high as man's.

An illustration pointing out the irony that the "savages" are more enlightened than the "civilized"

harmoniously complemented the hunting and diplomatic duties of men; both were equally valued. Within this framework of community responsibility, individual liberty flourished.

Six Nations Women Inspire Early Suffragist Ideas

The women's rights movement was born in the territory of the Six Nations in 1848. With the Seneca Falls Convention, women publicly formalized for the first time their vision of equal rights for women, a vision based on the authority and responsibilities held by Six Nations women.

While not an organizer of the Seneca Falls Convention, Matilda Joslyn Gage played an important role in developing feminist theory. Gage wrote extensively about the Six Nations, especially the position of women in what she termed their "matriarchate," or system of "mother-rule."

Spanning a twenty-year period, Gage introduced readers to the Six Nations in articles published in the *Post*; the newspaper she edited (the *National Citizen and Ballot Box*); and her most comprehensive book, *Woman, Church and State*. She explained the form of government of the Six Nations and their confederacy of peace.

When New York State legislators considered a law to force voting rights on Six Nations' citizens in 1878, the Council of Chiefs from all six Nations of the Confederacy met and refused citizenship in New York State. They were citizens of their own Nations, the chiefs pointed out. In May 1878, Gage wrote an editorial in the *National Citizen and Ballot Box* titled "Indian Citizenship" in support of the grand council's decision. Her clarity of understanding of Native nation sovereignty is a source of wonder to Native people today.

> Our Indians are in reality foreign powers, though living among us. With them our country not only has treaty obligations, but pays them, or professes to, annual sums in consideration of such treaties. . . . Compelling them to become citizens would be like the forcible annexation of Cuba, Mexico, or Canada to our government, and as unjust.

In 1893, Gage was given an honorary adoption into the Mohawk Nation's Wolf Clan. She received the Wolf Clan name *Ka-ron-ien-ha-wi*, meaning "She who holds the sky." That same year, she was arrested for voting for school commissioner, a state office. The New York State suffragists had won the right to vote in local school board elections. Gage tested whether the law could be extended to the state commissioner. She lost. Denied this voting right in her own nation, Gage's Wolf Clan sisters at the same time were considering giving her a political voice in her adopted Nation.

"Mrs. Gage, with an exhibition of ardent devotion to the cause of women's rights which is very proper in the president of the National Woman Suffrage Association, gives prominence to the fact that in the old days when the glory of the famous confederation of savages was at its height, the power and importance of women were recognized by the allied tribes."

NEW YORK EVENING POST

"Tell the readers of the *Herald* that . . . they have a sincere respect for women—their own women as well as those of the whites. I have seen young white women going unprotected about parts of the reservations in search of botanical specimens best found there and Indian men helping them. Where else in the land can a girl be safe from insult from rude men whom she does not know?"

REV. M. F. TRIPPE

missionary on the Tonawanda, Cattaraugus, and Alleghany reservations, told to a New York City reporter

Chapter 4

Two Very Different Views of Women's Rights

By living within the Six Nations' land base and knowing about and sometimes making friends with the women of those societies, the suffragists saw a stark contrast between their rights and those of their Native counterparts. They described these differences in many of the speeches they delivered at women's suffrage conferences and in the opinion pieces they wrote for area newspapers.

A Woman's Right to Protection from Spousal Abuse

Elizabeth Cady Stanton was especially sensitive to the issue of divorce. She publicly and consistently called for a change in the law to allow women the right to leave loveless and dangerous marriages.

To contrast Indian-style divorce in an 1891 speech to the National Council of Women, Stanton called on the memoirs of Ashur Wright, a long-time missionary among the Seneca Nation that was part of the Six Nations Confederacy. He wrote:

> Usually the females ruled the house. The stores were in common; but woe to the luckless husband or lover who was too shiftless to do his share of the providing. No matter how many children, or whatever goods he might

Illustrations of a Haudenosaunee woman and man dated from the 1850s

have in the house, he might at any time be ordered to pick up his blanket and budge; and after such an order it would not be healthful for him to attempt to disobey. The house would be too hot for him; and unless saved by the intercession of some aunt or grandmother he must retreat to his own clan, or go and start a new matrimonial alliance in some other.

Alice Fletcher, another women's rights organizer, pioneer in the study of American Indian society, and respected anthropologist of that time, delivered a speech at the 1888 International Council of Women, which she titled "The Legal Conditions of Indian Women." In it, she pointed out to this international gathering of early feminists that if the physical abuse white women sometimes suffered during marriage happened to an Indian woman, the relatives of that woman would see to it that the offending man was punished. To drive home her point, Fletcher mentioned what was obvious to the white women in attendance at this meeting: they had no such protections under U.S. law.

One of the results of the Dawes Act of 1887 was the breakdown of each Nation controlling their own lands and the resulting U.S. citizenship given to Indigenous individuals. Alice Fletcher reported that Native women were concerned about what would happen to them when they became citizens. They feared they would lose their rights and be treated with the same legal disrespect as white women. In addition, they would also lose the protection of their relatives against any sexual and physical violence from husbands and other males. It was not only a woman's female relatives who would take up her cause. Native men's intolerance of rape was commented upon by many eighteenth- and nineteenth-century Native and non-Native reporters alike, many of whom contended that rape didn't exist among Indigenous nations prior to white contact.

Coming from a European tradition that legalized both marital rape and wife battering, it was difficult to comprehend a culture in which rape was not allowed. Living in a country where one out of five women are raped, according to statistics from 2010, it is tempting to believe—

as some individuals promote—that rape is biologically inherent. Our feminist foremothers knew better, since they knew women who lived in nations where men did not rape.

A Woman's Right to Her Children

Gage described the European and American traditions of denying a woman's right to her children as similar to the institution of slavery. She pointed out that if a woman had children while she was enslaved, those children became the property of the slave owner. Since women of that time in this country had no right to retain their names after marriage, whatever money they earned, or any property they had previously owned, it was totally consistent that they would also give up any right they had to their own children.

In contrast to this, Gage spoke and wrote about how Six Nations children were descended through their mother's line, not their father's. Since a married woman maintained control of all her possessions, if she separated from her husband, everything she owned remained hers. Her children stayed with her. If she died, they stayed with her clan family. A child born to a Mohawk Wolf Clan mother automatically was Wolf Clan. This was true even if she married a white man; her children were recognized as members of her clan and Nation.

A Haudenosaunee cradleboard and its use

Property Rights

Native women, men, and children all had control of their own personal property, an authority that was respected not only by the Six Nations, but by other Native nations as well. After the death of a Native woman, her possessions went to her children.

Alice Fletcher talked about property rights among the Indigenous women in the numerous Native nations she had observed. Touching a sensitive nerve, she recounted her personal experience with the Omaha Nation in her 1888 International Council of Women speech:

> At the present time all property is personal; the man owns his own ponies and other belongings which he has personally acquired; the

woman owns her horses, dogs, and all the lodge equipment; children own their own articles; and parents do not control the possessions of their children. There is really no family property, as we use the term. A wife is as independent in the use of her possessions as is the most independent man in our midst. If she chooses to give away or sell all of her property, there is no one to gainsay her. . . .

When I was living with the Indians, my hostess . . . one day gave away a very fine horse. I was surprised, for I knew there had been no family talk on the subject, so I asked: "Will your husband like to have you give the horse away?" Her eyes danced, and, breaking into a peal of laughter, she hastened to tell the story to the other women gathered in the tent, and I became the target of many merry eyes. I tried to explain how a white woman would act, but laughter and contempt met my explanation of the white man's hold upon his wife's property.

A similar story came from a French woman, Emma Borglum, who spent her 1891 honeymoon with the Dakota on the Crow Creek Reservation of South Dakota, where her husband (the brother of the principal sculptor of Mount Rushmore) was working:

One day I showed some astonishment at seeing a young Indian woman, in the absence of her husband, give two horses to a friend. She looked at me very coldly and said: "These horses are mine." I excused myself saying that in my country a woman would consult her husband before giving such expensive presents. The woman answered proudly: "I would not be a white woman!"

A Six Nations woman not only exercised property rights over whatever she brought into a marriage, but also over whatever property her husband gave her to sustain and maintain their clan family. For instance, when a man came home from a hunting trip, the food and furs he delivered to her were hers to use and distribute as she saw fit. If she decided to sell the furs to a trader, she was the one who negotiated a price for the furs, not her husband.

When feminists—with the support of their male allies—waged an uphill struggle to gain married women the right to control their own property and wages, they won in several states. Interestingly, Native law regarding property influenced at least one of these states. The first married women's property law in the U.S. was passed in Mississippi

in 1839. Years later, the Mississippi Bar Association explained that this unlikely Southern state became a leader in women's rights reform because of familiarity with the law of the Chickasaw Nation, whose homelands were within that state. Chickasaw law recognized women's right to own their own property. The vision of economic equality in marriage spread slowly across the United States, as married women demanded their financial independence.

Equality in Employment

U.S. women's subordinate position in marriage spilled over into the world of employment as well, as Elizabeth Cady Stanton and the coauthored "Declaration of Sentiments," delivered at the Seneca Falls Convention, made clear (see page 11). Four years later, in her first speech at the third National Women's Rights Convention (see page 13), held in Syracuse during 1852, Matilda Joslyn Gage pointed out the connection between lack of employment, unequal pay, and marriage by noting that when women are denied fair wages in the workplace, marriage becomes the only opportunity they have for a safe, secure lifestyle.

Alice Fletcher, talking with Native women

How different this experience was from that of Six Nations women, who were doing the respected, satisfying, enjoyable work that gave them economic autonomy. The anthropologist Alice Fletcher talked about her conversations with Native women who were well aware of their superior rights, saying that those women felt they had much more freedom as members of their tribes than they did under white law. As more Native men came under the rule of U.S. laws, they also recognized the rights their wives, mothers, and daughters would lose under those laws.

Chapter 5

Women Take Power

The ability to vote was an important tool that women in the U.S. could use to gain their rights. They believed that right was fundamental in a nation where the government was based upon the consent of the governed. However, our government believed otherwise. As Stanton pointed out in "The Declaration of Sentiments"(see page 11), American society was built on a European model that historically placed women under the domination of men. All state laws denied women suffrage in 1848, and in 1874 the United States Supreme Court ruled that those states had the constitutional right to do so. While they achieved individual local, school, territorial, and state suffrage over the years, women did not achieve their constitutional protection of the right to vote until the Nineteenth Amendment (see page 19) was finally enacted in 1920, seventy-two years after the Seneca Falls convention.

The National Woman Suffrage Association waged a campaign of civil disobedience, during which they broke the law (by voting), refused to pay their taxes (claiming no taxation without representation), and accused the government of failing to live up to its founding principle—that a government should be responsible to all the people

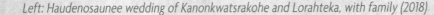

Left: Haudenosaunee wedding of Kanonkwatsrakohe and Lorahteka, with family (2018)

National Woman Suffrage Association Convention held in Chicago in 1880

it governed. Twenty-eight years after their first organizational call for the vote, Matilda Joslyn Gage outlined the suffragists' position in the "Woman's Rights Catechism." They argued that not only were they citizens governed under the Constitution and should have all the rights of citizens, but also that they should be able to exercise and enjoy the natural and fundamental rights that existed before governments were founded or constitutions created. They also felt that the job of the U.S. Constitution was to protect those rights.

The suffragists claimed they weren't breaking the law by voting, as some officials claimed. In fact, they asserted that the only people breaking the law were the individuals who kept women from voting. From Maryland to Washington Territory, from New York to Ohio, women by the hundreds, perhaps thousands, broke the law and voted in the decade after the Civil War. In Washington, DC, over seventy women

Sojourner Truth

Women who attended the 1851 Women's Rights Convention in Akron, Ohio, found their collective voice through the stirring words of Sojourner Truth, a formerly enslaved woman turned abolitionist. She rejected the stereotype of the fragile woman, so often used by men as an excuse to "protect" women from their rights. Presenting herself with a transfixing dignity, Truth declared that when enslaved, she had endured physical labor equal to that of many men while enduring the same punishment as enslaved men. She continued to speak out about abolition and women's rights until her death in 1883.

Mary Church Terrell was one of the first African American women to earn a college degree and was a national activist for suffrage and civil rights.

Suffragist Frances Ellen Watkins Harper was one of the first African American women to be published in the United States.

Women in Wyoming Territory voted in 1869 but because it was not a state, they could not vote for president.

marched to the polls in a single day, including a delegation of African America women. In New Jersey, 183 women attempted to vote over a four-year period. African American women voted in South Carolina, where the suffragist Rollin sisters wielded so much influence that their home was known as the unofficial headquarters of the then-progressive Republican Party. In Michigan, Sojourner Truth, the famous formerly enslaved suffragist, joined other women at the polls.

"The way to right wrongs is to turn the light of truth upon them."

IDA B. WELLS

By 1873, countless women throughout the country had presented themselves at the polls. Some had voted illegally and none had been arrested. However, when the government arrested Susan B. Anthony, the best-known suffragist in the United States at that time, both Gage and Anthony understood that this would be the government's test case. Organizing a whirlwind speaking tour, they brought their cause to villages in upstate New York, educating potential jurors in the county where the case would be heard. By the time Anthony went to trial, people realized that "taxation without representation" had surfaced for a second time as a burning issue in the country. The judge did not allow

"Lifting as we climb ... we knock at the bar of justice, asking an equal chance."

MARY CHURCH TERRELL

the jury to decide the case, nor did he consult them or allow them to indicate their opinion in any way. He found Susan B. Anthony guilty of voting, an act expressly forbidden to women under New York State law, and fined her one hundred dollars, plus costs.

Anthony refused to pay, protesting, "May it please your honor, I shall never pay a dollar of your unjust penalty. . . . And I shall earnestly and persistently continue to urge all women to the practical recognition of the old revolutionary maxim, that 'Resistance to tyranny is obedience to God.'" Her defeat was simply a skirmish. All around the country, women continued to go to the polls and brought suit against the voter registrars who refused to accept their ballots.

The National Woman Suffrage Association had counted on the government being true to its own principles. They believed it would only be necessary to point out that the government was not living up to the founding philosophy of the country for change to occur. What they had not counted on was the sharp moral edge of the church at that time. Ministers quoted the scripture of St. Paul, "Wives, submit to your husbands," to prove that women must be subordinate to men. Religious conservatives warned that the divine order of the universe would be overturned if wives stood beside their husbands at the polling place.

Mary Ann Shadd Cary was the first Black woman to publish a newspaper in North America. Both a suffragist and an abolitionist, Cary was also a teacher, an activist, and a lawyer.

When the NWSA allowed its chapters to segregate, African American women formed organizations such as the Phyllis Wheatley Clubs, which worked for Black rights and suffrage.

Ida B. Wells was an African American journalist, abolitionist, and feminist who led an anti-lynching crusade in the United States in the 1890s.

If women had always been under the control of men, the suffragists might have had to grudgingly admit that women's second-class status probably revealed a divinely inspired or natural order. An exception would throw into question this universal natural argument. The evidence of even one culture where women stood equal to men in decision-making authority would reveal the Euro-American practice of denying women's suffrage to be an arbitrary exercise of male power.

Once again, the suffragists did not have far to look for the example they sought. Their closest cultural neighbors, Six Nations women, possessed decision-making authority equally with men. Political rights were not new to these women. Their democratic government rested on the authority of women, as well as men. Female citizens of the United States had to break from their religious and political traditions in order to have a role in their government. On the other hand, women's political participation was traditional for the Six Nations, which believed the mutual authority of women and men was divinely inspired and necessary for maintaining the natural balance of the universe.

Ridiculed, labeled heretics, and arrested for the crime of voting, the courageous suffragists continued to believe in the rightness of their cause. They believed it was neither natural nor religiously mandated for women to be denied a voice in the decisions affecting their lives and the lives of their children.

Suffrage protesters outside the U.S. Capitol

"Woman is learning for herself that not self-sacrifice, but self-development, is her first duty in life; and this, not primarily for the sake of others but that she may become fully herself."

MATILDA JOSLYN GAGE

HAUDENOSAUNEE WOMEN
AN INSPIRATION TO EARLY FEMINISTS

Beyond Women's Rights

Beyond the ballot…
more than a vote in a system
driven by control

Our mothers saw people in harmony—
it stirred a remembering
of a time before the laws of church
and nation-state.

Sovereign women in sovereign nations
living beyond fear, beloved
not owners, but keepers of the land
not property, but sacred centers of creation

In a world where
everything is a part, connected
each valued and responsible to the whole.

Wiser women of older nations
remind us still today
that dominance, control, ownership
manmade, can be unmade.

Balance comes from honoring life,
living in Thanksgiving.
Wise women, living this vision,
we thank you.

*—Sandy Bigtree, Karen Kerney
and Sally Roesch Wagner*

Onondaga Nation women of the Eel Clan pictured above (left to right):
Deer Clan Mother Audrey Shenandoah, daughters Rochelle Brown, and midwife Jessica Jeanne Shenandoah.

Early feminists (left to right):
Elizabeth Cady Stanton, Matilda Joslyn Gage, and Lucretia Coffin Mott

Chapter 6

Mother of Nations

enied a political role in their own nation, the two major theorists in the women's rights movement, Stanton and Gage, knew and wrote about the leadership responsibilities of women in the Six Nations. Stanton described how the clan mother held the authority for choosing, keeping in place, and, if necessary, removing the chief that represented her clan:

> The women were the great power among the clan, as everywhere else. They did not hesitate, when occasion required, "to knock off the horns," as it was technically called, from the head of a chief and send him back to the ranks of the warriors. The original nomination of the chiefs also always rested with the women.

Voting is not a concept known to the Six Nations. The United States government takes the form of a representative democracy, with each citizen having a vote, and the majority rules. (Initially, of course, African American men and all women were not allowed to participate.) Among the Six Nations, decisions are made by consensus, and everyone must agree. It has been that way since the founding of the Confederacy over a thousand years ago. Voting does not exist. Rather, people speak and listen to one another, carefully consid-

Caroline Parker Mountpleasant, Seneca Wolf Clan

Women's nominating wampum belt

ering ideas, until they are all of one mind. There is a balance of responsibilities between men and women that allows consensus to work.

The Six Nations' worldview is based on keeping everything in balance. Women and men each have commitments that they must honor to maintain this balance. The clan mother heads the entire extended family that makes up a clan. Since the ancient founding of the Six Nations Confederacy, each clan mother has had the responsibility for carrying out the process by which the women of her clan select a male chief. The clan mother also has the duty of deposing the chief if he fails to perform his official duties. The man cannot become a chief or remain a chief if he commits rape, which is considered one of the three major crimes—theft and murder being the other two.

Balance also requires that everyone in the Nation has a voice, and decision-making is achieved by consensus in public councils. All questions, including the making of treaties and deciding on issues of war and peace, have always required the approval of both women and men. This ancient democratic government continues to this day, with clan mothers still choosing the chiefs. Even when the Seneca abandoned their traditional system and emulated the U.S. constitutional form of government in a desperate attempt to maintain their land—as had the Cherokee—the women still maintained their traditional authority over that land.

Gage was also strongly impressed by the influence the Six Nations had on the Founding Fathers. The United States government, she realized, was patterned after their Six Nations Confederacy.

The most notable fact connected with women's participation in governmental affairs among the Iroquois is the statement of Hon. George Bancroft that the form of government of the United States was borrowed from that of the Six Nations. Thus to the Matriarchate or Mother-rule

Artist Natasha Smoke Santiago (Turle Clan) is a proud member of the Akwesasne Mohawk Nation Territory. Her artwork is based on Haudenosaunee traditions, teachings, and family.

is the modern world indebted for its first conception of inherent rights, natural equality of condition, and the establishment of a civilized government upon this basis.

Congresswoman Louise Slaughter gave a long overdue thank-you to Six Nations women at the opening ceremonies of Celebrate '98, an event commemorating 150 years since the Seneca Falls Convention, the first official gathering to support women's rights. In acknowledgment of the Native practice of equality of rights, which modeled and laid a path for the early women's rights movement, the commemoration began with the First Words, the Thanksgiving Address, spoken in Mohawk by Wolf Clan

Mother Judy Swamp on behalf of the people of the world. Thus, history was made in the course of celebrating history, for the opening words were spoken by a member of the clan that honorarily adopted Matilda Joslyn Gage in 1893.

And so, has the woman's movement come full circle? Sisters in spirit with Six Nations women, Euro-American suffragists looked forward to a future inspired by the knowledge that women's rights were a lived reality, not just a dream. As Stanton said in an 1891 speech:

Three generations of an Onondaga Nation Eel Clan family: Jeanne Shenandoah with her daughter, Deionegatek "Honey" Myers, and new granddaughter Willow Tarbell.

Every woman present must have a new sense of dignity and self-respect, feeling that our mothers, during some periods in the long past, have been the ruling power, and that they used that power for the best interests of humanity. As history is said to repeat itself, we have every reason to believe that our turn will come again.

> *There is a word sweeter than mother, home or heaven. That word is liberty.*
> MATILDA JOSLYN GAGE

Marching in 1977 with Billie Jean King, Susan B. Anthony II, Bella Abzug, Sylvia Ortiz, Peggy Kokernot, Michelle Cearcy, Betty Friedan.

Awarded one of the first doctorates in the country for work in women's studies (UC Santa Cruz) and a founder of one the first college-level women's studies programs in the United States (CSU Sacramento), **Dr. Sally Roesch Wagner** has taught women's studies courses for 50 years. She currently serves as an adjunct faculty member in the Syracuse University Renée Crown University Honors Program.

A prolific author, Dr. Wagner's anthology *The Women's Suffrage Movement*, with a Forward by Gloria Steinem (Penguin Classics, 2019), unfolds a new intersectional look at the 19th century woman's rights movement. *Sisters in Spirit: Haudenosaunee (Iroquois) Influence on Early American Feminists* (Native Voices, 2001) documents the surprisingly unrecognized authority of Native women, who inspired the suffrage movement.

Founder and Executive Director of the Matilda Joslyn Gage Center for Social Justice Dialogue in Fayetteville, New York, she received the Katherine Coffey Award for outstanding service to museology from the Mid-Atlantic Association of Museums in 2012.

Photo Credits

"During the first suffragist wave in this nation, women were possessions, like a table or a chair. So violence toward them was quite condoned. The attitude has diminished, but it's still there."

GLORIA STEINEM

7th GENERATION

7th Generation is dedicated to publishing quality fiction and nonfiction titles for children and young adults.

American Indian authors provide cultural accuracy and exciting contemporary content showcasing the diversity of Native American Nations and Canadian Indigenous people.

NATIVE TRAILBLAZERS SERIES
Young adult nonfiction • Seven titles in the series

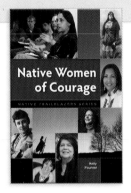

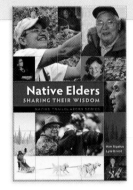

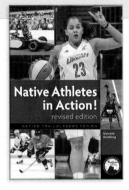

**Native Women
of Courage**
Kelly Fournel
$9.95 • 978-0-9779183-2-4

**Native Elders
Sharing Their Wisdom**
Kim Sigafus, Lyle Ernst
$9.95 • 978-0-9779183-6-2

**Native Athletes
in Action!**
REVISED EDITION
Vincent Schilling
$9.95 • 978-1-939053-14-5

PATHFINDERS COLLECTION
Young adult fiction • Twenty-two novels in the collection

Standing Strong
Gary Robinson
$9.95 • 978-1-939053-22-0

Finding Grace
Kim Sigafus
$9.95 • 978-1-939053-29-9

Found
Joseph Bruchac
$9.95 • 978-1-939053-23-7

Purchase these titles from your favorite book source or buy them directly from:
BPC • PO Box 99 • Summertown, TN 38483 • 1-888-260-8458 • Nativevoicesbooks.com

Free shipping and handling on all orders